TABLE OF CONTENTS

GIRL WORK

GIRL WORK

ZEFYR LISOWSKI

NOEMI

Published by Noemi Press, Inc. A Nonprofit Literary Organization. www.noemipress.org

Cover & Book Design by co•im•press

ISBN: 978-1-955992-04-6

"Any woman" "may already" "be dead"

—Alice Notley, *The Descent of Alette*

Don't you understand? It never ends. It will never end.

—Samara Morgan

AFTER I BECOME WELL, I THROW MYSELF INTO THE WELL HOLE

I spent years not remembering and once I did it was a riverbed.

It was a flood. It was highwater jeans.

I spent years trying to become a little saintly girl and threw my cell phone into the French Broad River.

Threw my cell phone down the well. Threw my throw-up in my hair.

Are you listening?

For a decade I devoted myself only to beauty. I worked at it, made a poem about my beauty. Made many.

What can we do with the beauty that's done unto us.

I've tried to be a better person and failed.

Do you remember the woods.

My favorite artist said, "I've tried to be a better person and failed" again and again. He said it on fifteen-thousand separate pieces of paper and this is why he's my favorite artist. He painted millions of girls and they all looked like me.

Blonde mop of hair. Thin angel of a dicklet. Torn bright rompers, the flood of them.

Do you remember the woods.

My favorite artist painted until he died, which refuses a logical end to it all.

And what you did in it.

Do you remember what you did.

In the woods I threw my cell phone down the well. There was no toilet nearby so I threw my throw-up in my hair. I laced up my boots and undid my entire body.

I don't need to tell you the ways I have failed.

I've tried to undo it all but all my little gender squeezing into the well hole and do you remember what you did.

It was an abattoir. It was a well hole. A grove of laurels. Your hands.

Maybe the better world smells like peppermint. Where we get justice for all the years we wore highwater jeans.

All the justices still seeping out.

The well, the water, the birds   calling

We are in the woods. I am talking to you. Look at my dazzling eyes. Do you remember what you did.

Maybe in the better world you are listening.

I throw my cell phone in the well.

Maybe there there's no remembering at all.

Maybe, after we give up on beauty, we enter a better world.

I've given up on beauty, but when did the betterness leave.

GIRL WORK

When I was eleven the man followed me on his bicycle across the whole town

I looked *pretty enough to eat* he said I was confused Called me

Treat of a girl *A gift a little gift*

Air thin and patchy Teeth small

Wearing my red-and-blue polo Just finished cutting a neighbor's lawn

Ten dollars in my pocket I didn't know any better Shirt sweat-stiff dirt-stiff

Tell me your secrets he said and I thought I was still doing work so I told him

Hair wraithed around me Apartment coated in smoke Clothes cigarette-wet

His mouth hiding a smaller mouth

Look—

I know how this sounds I wasn't even a girl yet I was content

I left once I saw the second mouth Trees lining the walk outside his house

It was a more obedient mouth

It was my mouth

GIRL WORK

Most of them tell me I'm pretty. The first
grabs me rough, but fucks like he's afraid
of something breaking. Another has
a scraggly beard and says how *special*
and *underappreciated* I am. *It must just kill*
you, he says. The one on Tinder asks
if I have a working cock. The ones under
the bridge in undergrad just tell me
to suck them off and rub their crotches.
The one with muttonchops was obnoxious
but his friends were cute. I'm fairly
sure at least three of them are girls now.
I pass out when the one with the graying
beard is inside of me
but he holds me afterward anyway.
Another one insists we fuck to the
Greatest Hits of Tom Petty. Isn't there anything
else you can put on, I ask as he cums into
a sock. The turtleneck one is super
excited to show off his top surgery and
whimpers during orgasm. The one with
the weird goatee smells like lavender
and has a guest bathrobe the color

of sunlight. He cries before he cums.
I didn't ask why. Now it's winter. Now it's
summer. Now it's summer again. The one
from OkCupid only needs me
for a threesome with his girlfriend. I
still say *maybe*. I don't know what
I want, but have I ever? The car roof is down
and my partner's driving, stereo humming
Tom Petty—*Full Moon Fever*. We're both
in sundresses and Tom is singing,
I-I-I-I'm depending on you. The one
I met for drinks takes me back to his place
and we then sit on his futon for hours.
A breeze stirs through the car. My partner
is good to me. The weather is in the eighties.
She brushes the hair from my face
and lets me stop for water when I need it.
I am only doing this because I want to.
Your lips taste like peppermint.

GIRL WORK

In my sleep I dream of other childhoods
until I feel better   Mirror me has a more queer
haircut   no regrets   She spends
her teen years chopping things apart
She chops the furniture in the ranch house
into tinier pieces of furniture
She chops my father into a kinder father
She chops outfits into a tote from Anthropologie
and pays for them with a shiny chopping card
This is a basically feminist act
Chopping past events into triumph
Chopping men in half like it would change anything
I am eighteen I am twenty-four
A wind from nowhere   nails freshly crimson
Look at me   I know what it means to be afraid
I don't sleep at night   She does

GIRL WORK

After becoming transacted, I decide to make myself
an availability.

I sleep with one hundred tiny men, all of whom
are identical.

I'm a good girl: I take my tablets as prescribed, fold
my body

into increasingly intricate arrays. Like the story of the girl
found at

the bottom of a well, I eventually become
a burning.

Do her bones clack like glass? Does the bag stay fixed
as she struggles

to breathe?
I measure the distance between hips as a way of feigning

knowledge and stroke their little beards.
A film, damp and cold. VHS. Childhood.

We were beautiful, and nothing happened.

What can this hole be but a home?

Foot slick with well water, dripping.

CRAZY4CRAZY

OR, PHARMACOLOGICAL SOLUTIONS FOR PERSONAL PROBLEMS

Redeem, says my favorite Robert Hayden poem,
rend me and redeem. For years
I took it as quiet gospel. I rent,
cut ribbons out of myself in the hope
that if I punished my flesh enough,
the quiet murmurs inside my throat would cease.
Theories of attachment-based distress
often trace the source
back to a fundamental lack,
but I was loved in my mother's arms,
loved at the bottom of my father's glass.
I was loved by friends when their parents were asleep.
I was loved so much the doors in my house didn't have locks.
I was six years old. Love permeated me,
and gently cleaned up afterwards.
I could list over a half-dozen medications
I have put in my body, and once did. I dreamt
of a poem titled PHARMACOLOGICAL SOLUTIONS
FOR PERSONAL PROBLEMS,
but that's not quite right—I refuse to believe
in the neutrality of science
or the personal, although I do believe

in problems. Instead, I trust
in the collective, or maybe persistence. The last
relationship I was in, I persisted.
We were both transsexuals.
We were both women deemed "crazy."
She said, *I'm at a rock bottom now*,
and we broke up three
days later, a frozen bouquet of expectations.
What is our responsibility to others
when our responsibility to ourselves
has been yielded away?
It's tired to say trans people
have higher rates of mental illness,
but I'm compelled to say it anyway.
I'm compelled to do a lot of things.
When I was six years old, I washed my hands
until red seeped from the palms.
This was a source of stress for my parents,
until they were compelled to hand me a book
every time I wanted to wash myself.
Then, it became a joke.
Her problems went away with reading,
my mother said over glasses of vino.
And it actually was a bit funny,
in that saying something objectively wrong is funny—
which my other girlfriend of many years
doesn't think is funny at all. *It's just wrong*,

she says, its own sort of joke.
In the middle of winter I broke
into the botanical gardens in early evening.
I wasn't sure if the security presence I feared
breaking into the botanical gardens in late evening
was real or not.
In the limp sun, I saw the crocuses
shattered by frost several times already,
budding bodies crumpled on the ground.
Every time I see a flower bud brave the trembling
warmth of a seasonal upswing, my heart sways.
Get back inside! I murmur. Anyway,
it was our third date, we were just about
to separate. The cops
showed up and escorted us off the premises.
It hurt, and it felt like coming home.
After I got out
of the psych ward, I took my bracelet, security
stickers off my phone and laptop, my journal
notes, collaged them together. I scrawled above:
love yourself, a motto insulting
in its simplicity, a punchline
drawn into the joke.
In the psych ward, the only view
out our windows was another psych ward,
shuttered, meaning: *what replaces the old is the old.*
This motto is more satisfying—as in *seems true,*

not *is reassuring*. In the relationship,
the previous girlfriend was beautiful,
yes, but I'm beautiful too. When fucking,
our hair snared together into a mass
the palette of a 2000s scene kid—
my shock of almost-bottle blonde, her
thatched auburn. She was rich, more familiar
with the workings of psychiatric
confinement than I.
A partial list of the things that brinked me
to institutionalization: our breakup.
Other girlfriend's COVID diagnosis.
My own economic precarity.
A bad shroom trip.
After discharge, I collected my things,
went home, and promptly had my appendix removed.
It had perforated several months earlier—another
shaky cause. My twin experiences,
the appendix perforating and the psychiatric hospitalization,
were both firsts for me, but not for those I dated.
This raises the question: what solidarities
do we prioritize while in love?
I don't think rich people are "crazier"
than everyone else. But their horizons
of available treatments are wider.
There can be a selfishness in taking care of your needs
at the expense of others', and sometimes I respect it.

Class is still a primal violence.
Once, while in a hypomanic episode, I dreamt
of a joke: three men dressed
in differently colored attire and a "murder-thief"
named Slatvinsky. An identical me approached us,
cocked her bobbed blonde head.
Which of these men is Slatvinsky? she asked me.
Before I could answer, the punchline:
None of them! While you were busy thinking,
the real Slatvinsky crept up behind you, whispered
"goodbye" in your ear, slit your throat, and took
all the valuables out of your pocket!
I woke to her cackling,
a roommate's cat yowling for food.
I suppose there's meaning in a transsexual
dreaming murderous other selves doing
what she couldn't do herself.
But I reject psychoanalysis
as insultingly patriarchal. Dreams merely
satisfy me—as in *seem true,* not *are reassuring.*
Now I tell the dream-joke at parties
and pay close attention to who laughs.
Here's another joke: my father chewed
peppermint gum so maybe that's why, even now,
I can't stand the scent. This isn't
about sex. Other things also hurt, and some
can be self-care too. Anyway,

I socked myself in the stomach, skipped
meals with an unnamed fury
until the murmur inside me became a cat's yowl.
Throughout all of this, the girlfriend lied,
the kernel of pettiness embedded here—other lovers,
secret girlfriends, her capacity
to be present. Towards the end, whenever
I talked to her, she'd say, *I'm at rock bottom now*,
and stop responding to texts.
What is our responsibility to others
when our responsibility to ourselves
has been yielded away?
I always scoffed at trans couples
with *t4t* etched on each other's arms,
but here I am devoting my life
to *crazy4crazy*. Am I so different?
In the psych ward, one of two refrains was
I want to get better. The other was
I want to get out, and my sympathies
were always with the latter camp.
We didn't share meals because of the pandemic,
but traded gossip. When the girlfriend
and I were together, the only things we did were
smoke weed, watch movies, and fuck,
which I now realize isn't a lot to build on. Maybe
the question isn't one of solidarity, but selectivity:
who is best equipped to show up in a crisis?

Those have been the other "crazy" people in my life—
but never the rich ones, regardless
of how much I needed.
There's a selfishness in them perhaps
inseparable from self-preservation.
I'm speculating. When my appendix swelled up the first time,
it felt like a bud emerging prematurely from the cold ground.
I spent days in the hospital and wondered:
Is this what being in a psych ward feels like?
In the dream, before she told the joke, other-me
reached out and embraced me-me with all her weight.
The answer, if you're wondering, is yes:
the beds, the gowns, the grippy socks, the waiting around.
Maybe the question is really one of redemption:
how can caring for one another supplant
a lack of care for oneself?
In the dream, I practiced a love despite violence,
and then told a joke with violence. In a lover's
arms, or over drinks with a close friend
on a drizzly day, there's a safety in which
I'm still myself. Maybe that's a better way
to think of the collective: a care.
Let's lay out our picnic spreads and dinner knives.
Let's share a meal. Let's cut up a whole-ass loaf
of sourdough. Maybe we can build our responsibilities
back up, together. Maybe, just as
I love pettiness, I can love abundance too.

Your tongue tastes like lavender.
Our pockets are empty. I'm out.
Meet me here. Redeem.

POEM WITH DEAD GIRL IN IT[1]

An anamorphic

"Let's play a kissing game" he said

and I didn't
even have to say
anything —I
loved *he said* being
in middle *"I w* school bec
ause my hes *ill* itation trans
formed into some *tell* thing m
o re elusive. *you* When his h
and d *little fag" wit*
o w n *h his hand in*
m y p a *mine we wat*
nts *ching* Twin P
he says h e eaks *under t*
lov es when my *he still a bi*
ton gue *tch how*
was tasting of *much a ho*
blood I was *me how*
a bitc *much a*
h his *home*
to
ngue a body
—find it— much

much

a home

1. To be read twice—once normally, once tilting down the page and squinting as in a Magic Eye®. Are you listening. Do you even know what you did.

RAPE FANTASY

The fantasy is that nothing actually happened. I waited weeks for our first date, full of anticipation, swallowing loudly at every encounter—the hallway, the classroom, the patch of woods behind campus. He gave me food I didn't have to pay for and slipped several fingers inside of me, *The Princess Diaries 2* on his dorm room TV. He talked about *how strong* he was and how much I *couldn't leave* and how I'd *take it* and then slept on the floor, worried I didn't have enough room on the bed. Body a root system at my feet. His beard like tiny teeth.

When I left in the morning, I looked three times before crossing the street—mountain roads sleek with rain and ribbon-like. I walked home in the fog. I didn't call my mom. The fantasy is that this happened how I remember it. He didn't call afterwards. He was polite. I walked past my house three times that morning without even seeing it. I took a shower but it didn't come out. The trees this time of year are so pretty. I'm changing only because I want to.

TO BE A GIRL IS ALWAYS TO BE A DEAD GIRL

And all these girls talking together. All their tiny breaths
of air, stupid eyes, fingers in wells or locked doors or narratives
that don't belong to them.

When was the first time you felt a hole inside? Felt
the hole widen? Felt the thick linoleum of the kitchen against your stomach?

Are you listening to everything coming out of my pretty-girl mouth?

His hands were like grass. No, they were like peppermint.

His dead, his girl.

When I remembered, I saw a hallway
filled with it all—

and then it happens again.

GIRL WORK

After the schoolyard incident   meanings blur
Average temperatures rise worldwide
My body luscious
Who wouldn't consume me
My gender is scrumptious
My pronouns are eaten/ate
I love the way my hair looks in this light
Apocalyptic   you know?
What's the opposite of being ruined?
The oceans have swollen three inches in our lifetimes
I cover my hands with salt
The news anchor says my body is a seaside
I can deny others' blame for anything
After it happens   I sit on the breakers
This is what I'm trying to tell you
My disassociation becomes statistical

Yes things are getting worse

Yes the subway flooding with people

Yes drought   Yes crying scientists

When I lost my dad I thought

Why am I not crying more?

This is a common narrative I learn

Things are consumed every day

I fling my body into the water

The anchor moves onto another story

I don't talk about loss much

The water is still rising

GIRL WORK

He called me. He did what he was supposed to. He smelled like lavender. He didn't call afterwards. He w
as polite. He wasn't my father but someday was someone's. He said nothing. He unbuttoned his blouse. He
threw me to the bed. He unbuttoned his shirt. He greeted me (the girl) in his bed. He moved his wealt
h (the girl, the dollar) around and around in small piles until he grew tired. He wore a bathrobe. He wore
a tee shirt. He wore a pair of jeans, said he was a big man, didn't ask for it. But he moved closer to me an
d the girl. He was kind. He was safe. He showed me the movie about the girl at the bottom of the well. H
e showed me the movie about the girl at the bottom of the well. He showed me the movie about the girl a
t the bottom of the well

He called me. He did what he was supposed to. He smelled like lavender. He didn't call afterwards. He w
as polite. He wasn't my father but someday was someone's. He said nothing. He unbuttoned his blouse. He
threw me to the bed. He unbuttoned his shirt. He greeted me (the girl) in his bed. He moved his wealt
h (the girl, the dollar) around and around in small piles until he grew tired. He wore a bathrobe. He wore
a tee shirt. He wore a pair of jeans, said he was a big man, didn't ask for it. But he moved closer to me an
d the girl. He was kind. He was safe. He showed me the movie about the girl at the bottom of the well. H
e showed me the movie about the girl at the bottom of the well. He showed me the movie about the girl a
t the bottom of the well

He called me. He did what he was supposed to. He smelled like lavender. He didn't call afterwards. He w
as polite. He wasn't my father but someday was someone's. He said nothing. He unbuttoned his blouse. He
threw me to the bed. He unbuttoned his shirt. He greeted me (the girl) in his bed. He moved his wealt
h (the girl, the dollar) around and around in small piles until he grew tired. He wore a bathrobe. He wore
a tee shirt. He wore a pair of jeans, said he was a big man, didn't ask for it. But he moved closer to me an
d the girl. He was kind. He was safe. He showed me the movie about the girl at the bottom of the well. H
e showed me the movie about the girl at the bottom of the well. He showed me the movie about the girl a
t the bottom of the well

POEM ONLY ABOUT BEAUTY

It collapses
the boundary
between thinking
and feeling Kat
tells me over too-sweet piña
coladas. I'm hungry
as usual. Lonely, threaded
with want. It's snowing.
My body, it's numinous.

○

I know I'm beautiful. I know this
because people tell me I am beautiful.

In a closed-door meeting in North Carolina,
a professor compares me to Greta Gerwig.

My first therapist in New York tells me
I look like the famous trans child

of a glamorous pair of local celebrities.
At an academic conference in Toronto,

a painter says I am incredibly
pure looking,

slides his hand softly
over mine while saying so.

Pure. Good. Whatever.
To be beautiful: to survive.

○

I've made my beauty. It suppresses
everything that's not my beauty.

I suppose most people must see
their noting of it
as a benevolent affirmation.

This person is striving
toward womanhood, so I'll tell her
what woman she looks like.

Drew Barrymore. Uma
Thurman. Michelle Williams.
Have you ever hid

your body from all that created it?

This is not an invitation.

A blanket of actresses, these skins.
A golden, phosphorous-pale field.

○

Fall passed over the city this year.
It shouldn't have been a surprise.

Leaves frosted overnight.
Every day I fail

in my attempts to write
about what most

people call "pretty":

A bird bobbing
its crested head. A man

scraping trash from the side
of the curb, snow settling into dirt.

This too is a kind of legacy.

Of course I can walk over to your place—
I'm putting on my makeup as we speak.

Is there anything else
you want to know about me?

I'm listening.

○

When I turned tricks, fresh out of undergrad,
my beauty's proximity
to other, more enfranchised beauty—

oh, men couldn't get enough.
Celebrity this.
Celebrity that. *You could be*

an impersonator,
they'd say rubbing one
out, *show me your tits*.

A sort of mother,
benevolent camgirl
next door, a hole.

Let's say I relished
these comparisons—
the way a thing can hurt
but affirm at the same time.
The smell of cedar before
it subsumes the senses.
They tipped me, of course.

Why am I telling you this?
I made my money. I was *beautiful*,

they said—
a pin-up princess.

A blonde girl but,
you know, less.

○

To be consumed, unencumbered. Numinous.

My beauty takes and takes all that's given to it.

I turn on the webcam and keep working.

A house. A yard. *Do you know what you did.*

○

Years ago, dinner with my partner in the park—boysenberry tea, nettles and agave—a feast for one and a half. I practice not eating with abundance. Drunk off approval, I drink myself thin. I drink myself shapeless. I mold my holes into an invitation generous as a ribcage. Twenty-two and foolish, there is no one I behold to more than myself—ensnared with availability, my body blossoming into an endless grinding machine. The more I punish myself, the more beauty I am allowed. This is how it works, acted on by a violence I don't even know to name yet. An expansion of territory unaware I owned. I am shaped by the wallet, bank account, shade of hair, skin, eye color particular to me. An accumulation unencumbered.

Beauty's reach is everywhere, and I don't even know what I'm doing. I buy a hard cider. I buy an eyeliner. I receive another compliment. My hunger grows. Are you there? Are you listening? I want to annihilate everything unanswered.

○

In other words: I buy a Fenty stick,
brush it cross my lips, walk
to work. Serve a coffee, smile,
buck fifty in the tip jar.

By the end of a shift everything
becomes dark, body sore from all its work.

Your hair's incredible customers say again
and again. *Is it real?*

The lights of the café click off.

○

I can't perform sober, so I buy some weed. I buy
a better vibrator. I bide

my time waiting for men to log on.
On Seeking, all the profiles say *trans only*

or *no trans allowed* I quit several
months later and can't

bring myself to fuck for weeks.
I take a nude, paste purple heart emojis

over the chest, post it online. I watch
a movie on Netflix and my ex coos,

points at the lead, *She looks just like you!*

Well water. A horror film. A blanket of
flesh, soft and warm.

I dream about men dying for months.
This, too, is a kind of beauty.

○

The secret about me: everything I write
is about beauty,

how I want it
flung from me like a damp rag.

I want to tear it out,
my red-toothed hunger. I want to tear it

from the clerk at the Rite-
Aid, scrape beauty off her soft pink

nose. Then the eyelashes. Then the gums.
To be beautiful, this country tells me,

is to consume and never stop.
I want to collect it all

in a hefty bag by the river
and hold it under til its fingernails

are ruined. Til its hair is long and stringy.
Like everything else,

beauty bears the violences making it.
An alabaster skin. A fuckability.

Put down every cent given me.
Open my eyes.

Scribble out
what everything gorgeous has awakened.

○

He makes me
vegan alfredo and we paint
our nails periwinkle after
finishing. Now I'm laid down on a duvet,
door locked, horror movie queued up.

            It's 2017. The lights shudder off,
barely present. There is no invitation
here. There is nothing
but our beauty—

○

An ex stopped eating in childhood, never
starts again. Here's a beautiful thing,
a small stone. Here is another.

The river by my mother's
house always bubbles
over its banks, ruining her small
patch of azaleas. It happens
again and again, and she never

moves the flowers. Have you noticed me
listening as you talk? It's because
I care. I look. I brush my teeth.
I'm focusing my beauty

into being a kinder, more patient person.
I do a trick. I practice my breathing.

My body aches.
There is nothing patient about any of this.
I do not wish to be beautiful, but it has been done to me anyway.

In the end, there's only work.

POEM ONLY ABOUT BEAUTY

It happens in the bathroom it happens in the
park it happens
in the man's house it happens in the
second man's house it happens
in the coffee shop it happens on the laptop

It happens in the museum it
happens in the painting it happens
in the woods it happens in the
park it happens in the car it happens
in the bedroom it happens in the child
hood bedroom it happens in the child
it happens in the child it happens in the
child

Take it Take it Take it You're so hot You're
so tight Hello hello hello So sweet so fis
like a real girl like a strawberry

When he touched me he kept touching
and I know my body is beautiful I kn
ow he is beautiful I know my body is
touching me is beautiful I know beaut
y's real I know there is a poem and the
re is his body and the only thing I kn
ow is beautiy is there only is beauty

My bruised skin my bruised eyes
my bruised fingers my toes your
toes your tongue it happens in the
ear it happens in the tongue chattering

A painting of a girl with a penis A painting of a
girl with wings and a penis a sculpture of a man
who is masturbating a picture of a famous film
star a man who is masturbating a girl with a penis

Are you a muse Are you a muse Are
you a muse are you a muse are you
a muse are you a muse

After it all, what do we have but our beauty?
After it all, what do we have but our beauty?
After it all, what do we have but our beauty?

GIRL WORK

My tongue does unforgivable things.

I am standing in the museum and I am speaking with it. I am stealing a selfie with a friend in the museum mirror. I am standing in front of a robot arm that is masturbating.

I will not deceive you.

The average lifespan of a trans, depending on one's source of information, is either twenty-seven years old or thirty-five years old or forty years old.

My friends all joke about this statistic. *I am almost at my lifespan*, says a boy I dated three years ago. He is twenty-four when he says this.

Of course.

Of course, averages are tricky.

A *trick* is a deception, and is also a man who employs the services of a loose woman.

The movie *Trick,* which I have never seen, is about two gay men living in New York City who fail to have sex.

They fail in kitchens, apartments, public parks.

I have failed at many things but, even in New York, even as a gay not-man, sex comes naturally to me.

You are so gorgeous, a man says to me selling peanuts from a cart. *You must hear this all the time*, a man says to me at work while eating an apple.

The masturbating robot arm moves up and down, up and down.

My first roommate in New York City did not say these things to me. He was poz, and mainly stayed in his dark bedroom, posted on Facebook about ACT UP. Wrote threats to me in Sharpie on our shared bathroom mirror.

The movie *Trick* came out in 1999, after the *New York Time*s declared the AIDS crisis "over."

On the newsstands, in the streets, elsewhere.

My first roommate hated the movie *Trick*.

Our apartment was disgusting, perched on top of a bus station in Bay Ridge, windows smeared with exhaust. It sickened me.

The retch of exhaust. This is what sickened me.

As a trans, I am used to the notion of being sickened. For instance, I never helped my first roommate with anything. Instead, I walked the long green tangle of boardwalk, silhouetted against the Verrazzano Bridge.

The numbers I've cited above, the life expectancies of a trans, are, ultimately, deceptive.

Deception is a funny thing.

For instance, it was still legal in New York State until 2019 to claim you were deceived by a trans person as your defense in the trial for their murder.

It is legal to claim this in thirty-three states in this country.

I was going to cite some examples of trials that used this tactic, but began to panic.

A more whimsical kind of deception can be found if you are in the museum. Going down the stairs, you come across a masturbating robot arm tucked away in a stairwell. You have been deceived: you expect a stairwell, and find a stairwell with a robot arm masturbating nothing. Masturbating a ghost.

I have given you several examples to ensure you are familiar with the concept of deception.

To return to my main point, the life expectancy of a trans is as low as stated because of several factors.

One: medical complications. HIV/AIDS, but also various cancers, a mutual distrust of doctors.

Two: suicide.

Three: murder.

When I lived in North Carolina, a neighbor who was not trans was murdered. Her death was all the papers talked about. Weeks.

Months. Her pale face fluttered in the newsstands, flickered in the TVs.

When a trans person is murdered, this does not usually happen. Usually no one talks about a trans person's death unless they themselves are trans, or they want to appear compassionate to an observer.

The news platform *Democracy Now!*, for instance, always covers transgender death. Amy Goodman shakes her heavy cisgender hair at each news item, blinks tears from her creased alabaster skin.

Mainly these murder victims are Black women who are sex workers, or women in the Global South who are not white who are sex workers.

As such, the lifespan of a trans, if you attempt to apply this information to all transes, is a deception.

I walked the Verrazzano Bridge every evening, illuminated in the floodlights.

I am of course myself a white woman, who has only occasionally done sex work.

I didn't mind the sex any more than I minded the work, but it was still work.

The first time I did sex work, it was over the internet. A man with a nondescript username asked for my home address in all caps.

Shortly after this, I read a poem about having sex with my then-boyfriend, and an audience member approached me afterward to say how much he liked the "sex work poem."

It was a deception. He was tricked.

All of this is to say, my own life expectancy cannot line up with my statistical life expectancy. My own, actual life expectancy has to be unknown.

I practice saying this on dates, rolling it around in my mouth like a glove. *Unknown*.

My white skin, she makes so many speeches.

Now to return to the poem. You may have noticed me signposting my transitions in this way.

I am referencing a tactic from the Oglala Lakota poet Layli Long Soldier. She does it in her poem "38." Which is to say, I am stealing it.

"38" a poem about the thieving of Native lands by white interlocutors.

This is not a sudden change of subject. In many ways, as I understand, I am a walking deception.

My whiteness, it thieves multitudes. It cloaks itself in flesh.

I'm not interested in compounding the problem of racialized theft, but am interested in paying attention to the dimensions we—white people—grant our thievery.

To name what happens, nameless, every day.

I tell myself I steal because my gender has rendered me unstably employed, but it's far more likely that I steal because I can get away with stealing.

An academic book. A coffee. My alabaster skin, sinewed and sinewing.

My dress outside.

As murderers may know, there is nothing innocent in one's dress. My father, who taught me to steal, taught me this: *There is nothing innocent about you in a dress.*

A sinking in the stomach.

There is nothing here that has not been stolen. We stole and stole and named it here. Named it work. Named it us.

There is nothing beautiful in being taken from, but there is even less beauty in taking.

Here is a tree, a field. Two white gay men running in the hollow of Central Park. I am coming to my conclusion.

My long blonde hair—in hallways, in busses, in private places.

Now the news broadcast goes on. It consumes.

A man calls my name. Many men call my name.

There is nothing taken from me I have not taken in turn.

An empty arm, moving up and down through the city. The folds of the park, whispering.

I know I am beautiful.

Do you know what you did?

Do you know what you did?

CHARYBDIS

It began suddenly.

A balmy day in November. A shadowy tear on my mother's cheek.

I'm sorry, she said, *it's happening again.*

Her shoulders shake against the blast of the Subaru's AC.

I was a child when I started to notice it: her daughter. The gradual training of my hand onto the place above her back.

If I were to do it, it would be in the ocean.

It would be warm, the sun unyielding.

A bouquet of bone-bleach coral, a handful of pills. I would be at ease.

When I first noticed, it wasn't even the ocean at all, but a seasonal creep.

I trained myself quickly.

Have you been involved in criminal activities? they asked as I filed for my passport the first time, and rejected me thrice for my answer.

I was nineteen when the riot cops shoved us to the ground at the BP protest, and everyone I knew from that day lives with chronic pain now, whether they say it publicly or not.

At first, when my friend killed himself in the eleventh grade, he said he was in too much physical pain to live. I thought that was a good reason to do it.

But, as the Sphinx said before she ate all those people, you have to draw the line somewhere.

When counting the years, it's not a question of *when*, but *how soon*.

Picture me as a child: passing out in the doctor's office, the middle of the night, a cramped amusement park, the bathroom, the bathroom, the bathroom, once at the moment of penetration, in strobe-lit lines, wherever it became too hard to breathe.

(My foster brother worked a shrimp boat in Biloxi but stopped after Katrina shoved him underwater and it became too hard to breathe. He's a Tampa gig worker now, fixing amplifiers in the AC as his state gets hotter.)

The biggest rush in a protest is the horizon that opens up: the sudden surf drawing us away into the streets.

The biggest disappointment is the realization that the tide just comes back again.

After my sister died, my mother said she wanted to obliterate her loss in the sea.

Two years later, I was born.

In other words: if my mother did it, the water would be warm, and there would be no me.

For the past twenty-seven years, I've pictured the future my sister never saw: a hotter planet, a smaller beach.

I mainly keep living out of spite.

After the state shoved us to the ground, I told myself the repression meant we were doing something worthwhile. That doesn't mean the repression didn't work.

Now, when counting years, it's not a question of *when*, but *how soon*.

At nineteen, I masked up and Sharpied the Lawyers Guild # onto my sweat-slick stomach before heading into the streets.

And then, as an afterthought, in neat bubble letters below it:

KILL THE SELF THAT WANTS TO KILL YOURSELF.

As a child, I wondered why the ancient Greek navigators who knew about all those sphinxes and whirlwinds kept piloting to their deaths. But maybe that's it:

The joy of finding the least resistance for a way out. How if it happens to you, you don't have to do it yourself.

On the island, I'd dig into the dirt. Because we were below sea level, mud rose out of the ground until I was wet with slop.

My sister did the same thing, but pulled out scorpions on sticks, holding them up to crowds of children nearby.

There's nothing to be afraid of, she cooed. She was nineteen when the car crushed her to death.

An entire ecosystem echoes in the November heat until nothing is left.

Maybe the trees will do a better job of governing this planet, a friend says.

Our little boat circling downward, hefted open by the chop of the surf.

It is 1992 and my sister is not afraid. It is 2022 and I am not afraid.

To be disabled is to know your body has already been marked by its refusal to go along with the expected order of things.

When the lungs fill with water, the body rejects it at first. One scorpion, then the next, wriggling on the branch and dancing up my sister's arms.

Even if the repression worked, we're still left anyway. Bodies twined like branches in assembly.

A mouth opens first in protest, then hunger—then light.

On the streets in our beds with one another, flooding out like a promise. Flooding out like a whirlwind.

Here we are. Living, at last, until we don't.

GHOST STORY

My father didn't do anything, but that is my point—how we are haunted and haunt everything closest to us.

How many fathers did.

My clothes were gray. My clothes were green. My clothes were a distant mountain. I didn't want to write about a father, but a future father's tongue is in my mouth like a pufferfish and my jaw won't stop pop-popping open.

Isn't it funny. He wasn't my father, but someday he would be someone's. That's how the equation works.

The only thing I knew my father did was drink himself to death. I wore ash at his funeral. But how many fathers did instead. How long will this go on.

We have a campfire we built to sit around.

We wear ash, all us lovely taxidermied girls. We talk about our endlessness. Come back, come back from it again.

I could throw myself down a well hole and be done with it.

I could lie and say, *my father did this*, and write off all fathers. I could only watch videotapes and paintings where I saw my own little face, taxidermied into perfection.

The ghost story was that they all knew what would happen as they did it. *You can't feel guilty if you knew from the start it was wrong*, I heard another father say once.

(You can't feel guilty if you convince yourself they asked for it.)

In my shiny new taxidermied body, I am one of the best kinds of total disappointment for my entire family.

Everyone I love is a campfire burning on and on, licking their tongues, endless.

Isn't it funny. I walk to the bus stop. I walk to the convenience store. I walk further again and still see all the fathers.

I see the men who did this to me and I know—pop—pop—they will all be fathers.

POEM TO BE READ IN A WORKSHOP

[I'd like to use my workshop time—the approximately *x* minutes of it—to talk about power. Who is allowed to write, and why. A professor tells me in a one-on-one meeting that I write about my rape because I have a sick fascination with violence. (Because I am like the professor.) The professor misgenders me as he says this.

What does it mean for, say, a professor to only teach or reference white poets, or male poets, or straight poets, or cisgender poets? Or to only invite to campus the same? What does it mean for multiple professors to do this?

What does it mean that this is happening everywhere?

I have worked and worked and worked and the only thing that shows for it is hundreds of white pages that all look like me.

The professor worked and worked and every one of his pupils said the same thing—first one year, then the following.

Of course, the violences done to white bodies are, almost invariably, the least violences that are done at any given time.

But surely you already know this.

You're smarter than someone I'd take to believe in politics, says the professor.

Please do not pay attention to the shape of these letters against the white of the page.

Keep this in mind: I am writing about what has happened everywhere.]

REMEMBERING IS A KIND OF WORK TOO

In the ghost story I don't write,
the girl meets the ghost, the end.

Ghosts are always a way out—a wet end—
            in this ghost world I am wet
with kindness, dripping open from it all.

When I was a girl, my hair was child-length.
I hid all my bruises with her.

            —Why didn't you leave the school?
But I did leave, and nothing changed.
I left the home. Nothing changed.

In the ghost story, a girl
            crawls through the hole,

enters a room like hers
but worse: a man with a book
for a tongue. A woman with dripping hair.

            When I was a girl, I entered
a room like mine, but worse—

my father was there, with a gallon of wine.
            His face dripping. No, flushed.

He slurred his words. He moved closer.
In the story, the girl leaves
            the room but can't leave it behind.

—Are you expecting mercy here?
Grace, or kindness?

Even after I got out, even after,
it followed.

TO BE A GIRL IS ALWAYS TO BE A DEAD GIRL

The dogwoods put out their leaves
earlier each year—first
April, then March. Petals litter the ground.

Our losses sprout inversely, to the point we only know safety
by a lack—

fallen branch, absence of fear on the neck.

ON VAMPIRES

The man had a big cape, which is how we knew he was a bad man. Big house. Shiny teeth.

When hooking an earring through a hoop of cartilage, my eye snags the mirror and can't look away, trapped in a memory box.

He had a lot of ways to avoid facing punishment. Redirected wealth. Moved his urns of earth around. Ran a tongue across teeth.

The first rich man I ever met had sad eyes and shiny teeth. He was actually a boy. In his house in the swamp, he had everything.

The difference between having everything and having some things is overstated, but I will state it again and again.

The bad man got to hold onto everything because no one talked about his wealth. Or if they did, they said he was a *false-rich*. Said he was *just like us*.

The bad man had a cape or maybe a thick coat or maybe pale skin or graying hair or a tan.

The rich boy lived in a house in the swamp with everything, and everything he served was underseasoned but still tasted of garlic. Having dinner at his place, I couldn't believe it.

I am one of the good ones, he told me.

When I enter the house it looks like a big yellow mouth and I go and go again.

The thing about bad men is they always appear to the ones in power to be doing the right thing.

The boy's fingers. The boy's teeth. A billowing cape. A procession of women.

I am not interested in anything claiming its own goodness.

In the house in the swamp in the woods in his bedroom in my sleep, his wealth. It was everywhere.

GIRL WORK

And it happens again. And it happens again. And it happens again. He was six and I was four. And it happens again. He was seventeen and I was sixteen. And it happens again. He was nineteen and I was eighteen. And it happens again. He was thirty-five and I was twelve. And it happens again. He was a friend. He was a neighbor. He was a casual acquaintance, but always smiled when he saw me. And it happens again. His fingers were smooth. He grabbed me and they felt like a kiss. And it happens again. He kissed me and it felt like a grabbing. And it happens again. His bike wheels were large, and squeaked as they turned. His smile was large. His eyes were deep. And it happens again. We were children but it still happened. I was a child and it still happened. I was almost an adult and still it happened. And it happens again. And it happens again. And it happens again. And it

And it happens again. And it happens again. And it happens again. He was six and I was four. And it happens again. He was seventeen and I was sixteen. And it happens again. He was nineteen and I was eighteen. And it happens again. He was thirty-five and I was twelve. And it happens again. He was a friend. He was a neighbor. He was a casual acquaintance, but always smiled when he saw me. And it happens again. His fingers were smooth. He grabbed me and they felt like a kiss. And it happens again. He kissed me and it felt like a grabbing. And it happens again. His bike wheels were large, and squeaked as they turned. His smile was large. His eyes were deep. And it happens again. We were children but it still happened. I was a child and it still happened. I was almost an adult and still it happened. And it happens again. And it happens again. And it happens again. And it

GIRL WORK

1.

I was a child. I wore my child clothes. I watched movies and went home afterwards.

Hair long and matted. Body touched. And so on.

When I was a child, the boy showed me the movie, his eyes tiny pools of light. He showed me the movie about the girl at the bottom of the well.

Why is it so hard to write what actually happens.

The boy started the movie. The boy stopped the movie. When the movie was done, the boy climbed up and down the staircase like the girl at the bottom of the well.

Our house was small and smelled like cedar. I won't tell you what happened next.

The girl had, of course, a bad father. She had a farm problem. She had a little room she lived in, and I didn't see what was so wrong about that.

Nothing happened next but its shadow hung over every interaction the boy and I had after that.

But the boy did have a friend who loved to bite.

Loved to put the soft flesh of me in his mouth, boy tasting boy.

Everyone, someone said in the movie, *deserves a little room.*

The girl had two. She had her little room and she had the bottom of the well.

It was a sunny day. It was overcast. It was slightly cloudy, but we kept going.

The boy's friend took the soft flesh of me and placed his tongue upon it. Placed his teeth inside me. Made my arm his home.

My hair was long and matted. No one told me to take a hairbrush to it. They told me I was *a boy being a boy*. Actually, they told me I was *asking for it*.

In the movie, the girl doesn't ask for anything. But she does grow more dead, then less dead, then more dead again by the film's end.

She moves around, but she's still at the bottom of the well. She gets more or less dead, but she's still dead.

So many different kinds of dead.

His incisors were long and dazzling.

Years later, I read the book. In the book, the main character is a man. He loves to rape.

This is what you might call his "defining trait." He says to his quirky friend, *I have a secret. I raped a girl today*. He says it again and again.

2.

I read it because I heard the girl in the book was a girl like me. That she had genitals that stuck out instead of in. Used to love the smell of cedar.

In the book, a man discovers her genitals, rapes her, throws her down the well. This is how she dies.

This is of course not what happens in the movie. In the movie she is a young girl, hair matted. No one looks up her skirt or, if they do, it's when the theater lights flicker on and no one is around.

When the friend's friend who loved to bite pressed himself onto me, I knew it had been only a matter of time. He threw me to the bed. He said he was *a big man*.

In the movie the only man the girl knows is her father. Her father kills himself after the girl dies. The movie frames this as him dying because he was scared, but I think he died because he was grieving.

I read the book when my father was on his deathbed.

There is no grieving in the book, which makes it an incongruous read in the hospital. I signed in and saw my father. I read my vile book.

When my father died, I grieved—but less than I thought I would. This made me worry. I smelled the cedar. I looked at pictures of his face. I miss my dead daddy so much, still.

3.

In the movie, everyone thinks the girl is a girl. She walks like a girl, eats like a girl.

In the book, the girl is a woman, and she literally asks for it.

This is the girl's power, to make men first think she is beautiful—and then want to kill her. This is what makes it scary.

As we watched the movie, my friend didn't show his body to me and I was grateful. He didn't touch my hair. He didn't call me beautiful, hunger for my body. He didn't ask for it.

I have talked about beauty a lot. By "beauty" I mean that which causes you to become an object of fascination, and sometimes to be thrown into a well.

I can't imagine what it feels like to be thrown in a well.

When my friend with the dazzling incisors came over, my father let him in. His voice rattled the foyer. It fried our eardrums. It frisked our pockets. *Welcome*, he'd say. WELL, he'd say. COME.

A man who drank too much. Had a daughter who was dead. A deep voice that scratched the ceilings of the well.

I don't blame him for anything that happened.

Let me rephrase that. I used to blame him for anything that happened, and then he died.

My friend and I would get together and watch movies. The only one I remember was this one.

I wonder if the girl was terrified she was not beautiful. I wonder if she avoided brushing her matted hair to feel she could control whatever part of her life she could reach.

It might occur to you that I am not really talking about a book or a movie.

A ring is a kind of circle, but it also is a sort of promise that things will continue. I am trying to write something that rings true to what happened.

He sunk into my soft flesh and the movie wedged inside me like a stone.

At what point is a girl no longer a girl.

His dazzling incisors, the deep smell of cedar.

Have you ever fallen into a hole and couldn't get out?

The girl brushing her matted hair, sending her body to so many other people's bodies.

When she clatters up the walls of the well,
when she appears again in front of the man who killed her,

I'm sure she looks

beautiful.

GIRL WORK

Growing up I hungered for the taste
of sameness   So I stayed hungry
I ran miles each day   Petulant, I demanded gifts
but could not even love myself
Food turned to bark in my mouth
My dreams were thorned with ghosts
I sprouted hair & shaved off
hours in the bathroom   willing my ribcage to shrink
I called this *care* but who hasn't
ever made a horrible mistake in naming
I called this *beauty* but who hasn't felt fear
instead of awe at something uncrushable
When I was younger I was a wolf
I trusted the man because he was pink
He was practiced in being pink
& I thought could teach me the same thing

(I meant to say I was a girl but am trying

to seem more menacing than I am)

He tied me to his lips He held my wrists & told me it was love

The man was cruel & that was also the lesson

GIRL WORK

I pay my rent and go to the rent store

I buy a new shiny rent

I buy a tight-fitting outfit to tell myself I am rent

The weather shiny

The sun flecked with little bits of wealth

Hello I am looking for feedback and also rent

Is my body managed with sufficient affect

Has my poor been concealed craftily enough

Open your mouth and pour your riches onto me

Someday they will own this too

ARE YOU THERE STILL? OH. I DO, I DO, I DO.

It's the calluses I remember first, their gentle rub as you slide two
polish-chipped fingers inside me—
breath hot, slick fucked, dick sucked, stuck it in and stuck.

In the dark, we pillow princess,
bend backwards, shed skin, slip another, slip again—
shorn nude nothing

but the hue of your tongue and tooth. I want the thick
smell of armpits, your downy soft forearms, the gap
between your eyes, how you fix

your glasses when they creep down your nose.
Babe, I want you so bad there's nothing but beauty left.
I want it all: the curtain and the rod, the nothing

and the nothing that remains. I want to be crushed so hard
I come out dribbling. Joy still
a foreign country to me, but let's stay in your rinky-dink

sublet until its shoreline comes
into view. Hold me til your toes curl and tell me
there's nothing you wouldn't do.

GIRL WORK

Of course I smile   Of course I say *yes* and call him *a friend*   Of course my hunger allows
me a narrow channel of entrance   small desire stream
I am not telling you I am broken in my want   but I have been before
Waiting for a bruised arm to heal   Trading stories with coworkers   whiskeys neat
Breaking into public areas as an act of cute resistance
The summer that broke me was like any other
Water faucet sweet and cool   Air conditioner wet as a body   Mask taut against the face
          When he found me he said nothing
I still remember Look at me I am pretty and know how to work

I work in a higher pitch

GIRL WORK

And this is what I say to you. A girl is a kind of work. A body a kind of bird. A cage a kind of artwork.

When I saw the man's body I said, *Oh! What a beautiful body*, and feasted with my eyes. I fisted with his tongue. I tasted the salt of the rim.

His hands so very pink.

When I clipped the wings of my beauty, I put them in a lockbox and did not let them out until they were good and dead.

When they were good and dead the man's beauty became overwhelming to me.

I know the feeling of cramming your flesh into a closet for seventeen years. The hunger of being a dead girl in a sea of dead girls.

When the violations began to emerge, I was in my last year of college. Had just turned twenty-one.

When I started remembering all my violations I curled into a cage and didn't speak. I cried for fourteen nights straight. I didn't think of the beauty of his body, his lovely thickets of hair.

When I emerged from my stupor, I could only eat clementines, drink as many margaritas I could find.

I cried for fourteen nights straight and when I emerged, I hit my girlfriend.

We were walking in the woods after dark, cool mountain crick refracting splints of moonlight. We didn't hear any birds. I was thinking of what I thought before thinking of the beauty of his body.

When my thoughts were good and dead I was still thinking of his body, his warm pink hands.

We didn't hear any birds. There had been, according to the paper, a series of unexpected deaths. The birds had all left.

When I hit her my mouth popped in a sad *oh!* of surprise and I started crying and she did too.

It was a tiny hit. It was on the upper part of her shoulder.

We had packed peanut butter sandwiches and the plan was to eat them by the outskirts of the woods near where the birds had all left.

After my violations began to emerge, hands like wings filled my everywhere I looked. Flooded the hallway outside work. Flitted beside me between classes.

You're less present now, a professor said during a class on the witch hunts.

Are you still there? my boss at the gallery I girled at asked. Lips fluttering like a bird.

I didn't know why I hit her. I dropped my sandwich on the ground. I picked my sandwich off the ground.

The moon a thumbnail-edge of blood, staining everything a slight little pink.

I felt like I had been crowbarred out of a closet. I felt like my blood was replaced with something almost like blood.

The cage dangling against the edge of the woods, rattling like a little rib.

I didn't say anything, but of course we kept walking.

The woods stretching on forever, every dazzling orange leaf crunching beneath our Uggs.

We kept walking and I saw floating hands and I'm sure we both heard so much. The murmur of the creek, my crying, my girlfriend's crying.

When the beautiful man unzipped his body, I was still in high school and didn't know how to say yes.

So he said it for me.

My hands covered in snot and peanut butter, my girlfriend's hands covered in snot and peanut butter.

The moon so full one could feast on it. The sound of our breathing and the hoot of a wood creature. We were girls.

His hands were there too. He feasted on me.

The violations emerged, and something was taken over in me that I could not take back.

There in the woods, without the birds, you could hear it all.

POEM ONLY ABOUT BEAUTY

My favorite painting is a girl with a nubby little penis
looming over a meadow. Her wings are
dazzling, and every other girl nearby jostles

to look at this beauty. Before we broke up, my ex
said I was the most exquisite
person he knew, but I suppose most people

who notice me do so as a kind
of benevolent affirmation. Have
I told you yet about my endless

golden hair? The artist
in question called girls like me "peacherino,"
which is the cutest little threat I've ever heard.

I want it flung from me like a damp rag.
I want to tear it out. I want to tear it.
to collect it in a hefty bag

You're so beautiful. Oh my god,
you're so fucking beautiful.
Your hair's incredible, customers say
Your hair's incredible, and again. Is it really
A blanket of

A *fuckability*. A *fuckability*.A *fuckability*. A *fuckability*.
A *fuckability*. A *fuckability*. A *fuckability*. A *fuckability*.
A *fuckability*. A *fuckability*. A *fuckability*. A *fuckability*.
A *fuckability*. A *fuckability*. A *fuckability*. A *fuckability*.
Here's a beautiful thing. Here's another.
Here's another. Here's another. Here's another.
Here's another.Here's another. Here's another.
Here's another. Here's another. Here's another.
Here's another. Here's another. Here's another.

Well water. A horror film. A blanket of
flesh, soft and warm. Well water. A horror film.
flesh, soft and warm. Well water.
flesh, soft and warm.

thing. Here's another.
Here's another. Here's another.
Here's another. Here's another.
Here's another. Here's another.
Here's another. Here's another.

I dream about men dying for months,
This too is a kind of beauty.

Where are you going, bitch

Here's a beautiful thing. Here's another.
Here's another. Here's another. Here's another.
Here's another. Here's another. Here's another.

GIRL WORK (POP SONG)

Everyone's mother had a little house with a river by it, lived in the suburbs for the first time, liked the new Ke$ha album more than she'd think Cross-class relationships in the supermarket, boutique vegan products for her boutique vegan child When she had my sister my mom was fourteen and whn I was fourteen I had sex too, but wouldn't realize that was what it was until years later when a boy did it to me after I actually asked him to When I was fourteen I thought everyone was a friend I rode my little bike I listened to the radio I **tik-tokked** I **didn't stop** I **on the clock Dj blow my speakers up** and everyone's mother bopped along We liked Ke$ha because she had a song about fucking co-written by her rapist A song about dying co-written by her rapist A song about fucking a ghost co-written by her etc. Everyone's mother walking in the suburbs listening to the radio eating vegan sandwiches We liked Ke$ha because she made it easier to say not saying anything was okay When I was fourteen I didn't say anything to my etc. We ate vegan sandwiches and together he raped me But I did say "I'm not sure" I did say "maybe some other time" and he pulled me onto his vagina and stroked his chest The little river-stones of the suburb the manufactured sheeny pop beauty of it all

GIRL WORK

Even tonight and I am tired of this grief or guilt

I am gilled   The water   These holes

    I have nothing to tell you about the longings netted over me

A woman still says over omelets *I can "take it"*

Her lips   Our food

    Did you take it he said   *Did you take it good*

In my dreams   A shark swims iridescent with sunlight

    And I am beautiful again

Taking   everything   berobed with blood

There's a tide coming she says   Waters muddy with blood

Did you take it good

His teeth   His skin   His eyes

We were in public   And it continued

Take it

    Their eyes   We were on the beach

We were watched and no one did a thing

Eating omelets Slope of seashore

Sharks so lovely this time of year

There's a tide coming and he's here again

Across the dining table Across the bathing suit

Sandy-shored body

A fin A tooth *Take it*

Are you listening?

she asks

You're not here right now

Sharks glow

All continues

Here

Bodies draped across the table

Bodies clot the water

I close my eyes and nothing but bodies Happening again

We were in public

At the beach On the street In a convertible

I took it all It continues anyway

Teeth sharp Skin slick Eyes dark

(What do you do when a body is betrayed enough to not know its own name?)

Are you listening? she asks   *You're not here right now*

Diner clanging

Mouth smudged   Omelet gone

Take it all

Go—

Wade into the deep

Drown it til there's nothing left

AGAINST FORGIVENESS

Was not a monster—(His hands were soft)
Was not an abnormality—Was not just
"being a boy"—Had no reputation—
Had no warning signs—Was a brunet,
with soft hands—Had soft hands—
That's the thing about it, his hands
were soft. He'd stare and stare, touch
and touch, with the soft hands. He'd visit
me in my room, which was not an act of mercy.
Which was not an act of submission.
But his hands were soft and he'd ride
his bike over to me—His eyes were soft
and he'd show up pearled in sweat at my door—
I'd say, *How can I help*—I'd say, *I'm sorry*—
I'd say, *You've changed* and of course
I believed it every single time—Every
single time he would undo me and still
I said nothing—He would undo my friends
and still I said nothing—I don't even know
how many more he undid, but still I did
nothing—Let the merciful me
burn with the rest of it. His eyelashes.
His soft hands. Pushing me onto

the cold box-spring. Imagine it—Just
seventeen, skin goosepimpling with desire—
My lips parting—Preparing
to forgive again and again
and again until there was nothing left. Burn it all.
Even this. Burn this.

ONE FUNCTION OF THE LINE IS TO ORDER, ANOTHER IS TO CUT

And a tree bends in hunger for both.

You don't know how much I've wanted it,

how many times I've dreamt me open.

June. The blistering yolk of the highway.

July. A forest of bodies in marble and fieldstone.

Beloved, when your lips skip down my throat.

The puckers run and last for weeks.

A bough creaks. The line ends.

August. October. February.

We are different from most

women, my mother says. *We endure*.

SEXUAL HISTORY

It's 2013 & the forsythia pushes against the window it's 2015 & the air
conditioner is clanking it's 2021 & the bedroom lights are out, low slit
of a moon barely visible & we are both so wet.
Kindness doesn't always feel safe but still I love your spit-slick fingers,
ringlets dredging the brow, little thin scars around the hairline,
eyes swimming in hazel. There's a snowstorm so of course
we spend the whole day in & you eat me out three times, holding my body
afterwards like a flower coiled on the stalk.
I like your paint-chipped toenails, broad shoulders, small teeth.
You like everything about me so I sink myself in your arms & call it comfort.
I've done this thousands of times & there's a knack to it:
the first thing to not desire too much, the second to be unquenchable anyway.
Who am I fooling with my talk about restraint? I'm insoluble in my want.
When I ride you, a locket clicks shut & my flesh feels filled.
We submerge for so long our fingers prune & the center of me spills
into what's left tugging at the thread.

It's already almost over but tell me in my prettiest chiffon this can last.

Tell me in your best Prince impression you'd do *anything* for me.

The wind is yelping, & oh. Oh.

Touch me until the well turns over and flows past the horizon of our limits.

We're here now: grab me, ride me, ream me out

until we remember nothing at all.

POEM ONLY ABOUT GIRL WORK

I'm writing in a dark room. Maybe the body
of the poem is a child. Maybe the body's
finding itself, like it should have as a child.
Maybe there's no redeeming
or justifying what's been done to the poem's body—
now or as a child. Are you listening?
I skip dinner again, my most cherished habit.
I wish to talk only of pretty things, pretty
bodies. But there's a distance between naming something
and naming yourself.
I need you to know I'm writing because I miss you,
but I will never forgive what happened.
Poem, I don't need to tell you what happened,
but I'm finding myself in it even as we speak, as I write
again toward this body so many
have written on already.

All their comments, comparisons.

When does telling yourself you're pretty

cease to become a mechanism for staying

alive another day?

I'm writing this in my handheld

machine. I'm Venmoing

my friend for a slice of pizza.

My teeth are too long. I'm an animal.

Of course I care about every single word I hear.

Poem, ignore everything I say about myself—

thick hair, obscured genitals, all of it.

I'm standing in my bathrobe, reading the comments

section one more time.

I'm washing the filth off my face.

I'm holding on with a meanness

so abundant it could be taken

for grace. Poem, I don't know

what I think, but have I ever?

Now I'm standing up too quickly.

Now I'm stopping for water
when I need it. Now I am twenty-nine,
a sudden crush of flowers.
I'm here. I'm alive.
I'm in the bathroom
looking at you, mirror,
flesh bright and unbruised
against the frame—
air crisp as well water,
held,
                    unpretty at last,
by the great,
                    fucked,
flawed beauty
        of the whole.

NOTES

The Samara Morgan epigraph is from the American motion picture, *The Ring* (Gore Verbinski, Dreamworks, 2002)

Jim Elledge's book *Henry Darger, Throwaway Boy: The Tragic Life of an Outsider Artist* (Harry N. Abrams, 2013) was used in several sections of "After I Become Well, I Throw Myself into the Well Hole" and "Poem Only About Beauty."

"Girl Work [Most of them tell me I'm pretty]" owes a structural debt to Grey Vild's poem "M4T" (published in *Brooklyn Poets*, 2015*)* and interpolates one lyric from Tom Petty's song "Depending on You" (*Full Moon Fever*, MCA Records, 1989).

"Girl Work [In my sleep]" adapts a line from the ending of Ai's poem "The Boy" (*Killing Floor*, Houghton Mifflin, 1979).

"CRAZY4CRAZY" is indebted structurally to Elisa Gonzalez's poem "Consumerist Solutions for Capitalist Problems" (unpublished). The Robert Hayden poem referenced is "Bone-Flower Elegy" (*Collected Poems*, W.W. Norton, 2013).

"Bones clacking" from "Girl Work [After I become transacted]" is a phrase borrowed from Muriel Leung's poem "Mourn You Better" (*Bone Confetti*, Noemi Press, 2016).

"Girl Work (Pop Song)" interpolates lyrics from Kesha (fka Ke$ha)'s song "Tik Tok" (*Animal + Cannibal*, RCA Records, 2010).

Part of the visual design of "Poem Only About Beauty (Return)" is indebted to the typographic poetics in Aurielle Marie's *Gumbo Ya Ya* (University of Pittsburgh Press, 2021).

"Girl Work [Even tonight]" borrows "Even tonight" as an opening—and the idea of poem as propulsive device—from June Jordan's "Poem about My Rights" (*Directed by Desire*, Copper Canyon Press, 2007).

"Girl Work [My tongue]" is indebted deeply to Layli Long Soldier's poem "38" (*Whereas*, Graywolf Press, 2017).

The artwork described in "Girl Work [My tongue]" is from the Sarah Lucas retrospective *Au Naturel* at the New Museum from Fall 2018.

"Sexual History" interpolates Charli XCX's song "claws" (*How I'm Feeling Now*, Warner Records, 2020) and Prince's "I Would Die 4 U" (*Purple Rain*, Warner Records, 1984).

Several of these poems interpolate content from the American motion picture *The Ring* (Gore Verbinski, Dreamworks, 2002) and the Japanese novel *Ring* (Koji Suzuki, trans. Glynne Waley, Vintage, 1991).

ACKNOWLEDGMENTS

This book would not be possible without the work done in these earlier books for me:

-*Panther*, Brecht Evens

-*Indictus*, Natalie Eilbert

-*The Pervert*, Michelle Perez and Remy Boydell

-*I'm So Fine: A List of Famous Men & What I Had On*, Khadijah Queen

-*The Compleat Purge*, Trisha Low

-*Black on Both Sides: A Racial History of Trans Identity,* C. Riley Snorton

-*Directed by Desire: The Collected Poems of June Jordan*

Additionally, an earlier version of this book was centered entirely around Joyelle McSweeney's concept of the "necropastoral," and the space our bodies take inside of it. That book no longer exists, but one of the poems in here is a holdover from that project. Like a garlic head sprouting a shoot, this book would not be here without that earlier work.

Parts of the manuscript were written at Sundress Academy for the Arts, at the Lacawac LGBT Artists Residency, and at the 2019 Tin House Summer Workshop, in addition to in New York City, Portland, OR, Richmond, VA, and Philadelphia, PA; as with all of my writing, this book was produced with labor and time stolen from waged work as well. Currently, I sit and write on unceded Lenape land, & that theft must be acknowledged too.

Parts of this manuscript have appeared, sometimes in earlier forms, in *Black Warrior Review*, *Femmescapes*, *Foglifter*, *Hayden's Ferry Review*, *Michigan Quarterly*, *Muzzle Magazine*, *Nat. Brut Magazine*, *The Rumpus*, *The Shallow Ends*, *Split This Rock*, *The VIDA Review*, *Waxwing*, and *Wildness*.

Thank you to the first readers of poems in this book, in various forms: Maria T. Allocco, John Manuel Arias, Samiya Bashir, Catherine Barnett, Joey De Jesus, Joselia Rebekah Hughes, Cyrée Jarelle Johnson, Donna Masini, Jesse Rice-Evans, Stacy Szymaszek. Thank you, especially, to the trans women who were among this book's first and most responsive and incisive readers: Spencer Williams, Valentine Conaty, S. Brook Corfman. This book would be nothing without your generous time. Additionally, thank you so much to my blurbers, for seeing this finished book in all its complexity:

Cameron Awkward-Rich, Natalie Eilbert, and Cyrée Jarelle Johnson.

For my loved ones and lovers who nurtured, fed, and held me during the writing of this book: thank you as well.

To my Tin House Summer 2019 cohort (Team Bashir!), where many of these poems were first wrestled with. We, too, are a thing of beauty.

To everyone at Noemi Press for all their brilliant efforts, especially my editors, Sarah Gzemski and Diana Arterian, and book designer Steve Halle.

And for my mother, who first taught me that beauty and intellectual rigor were not enemies.

I love you all.